P9-CAU-069

GUINNESS W★RLD RECORDS

GUINNESS WORLD RECORDS™

EXTREME ANIMALS!

COLLECT & COMPARE WITH

FEARLESS FEATS
Incredible Records of Human Achievement

WILD LIVES
Outrageous Animal & Nature Records

JUST OUTRAGEOUS!
Extraordinary Records of Unusual Facts & Feats

DEADLY DISASTERS
Catastrophic Records in History

MYSTERIES & MARVELS OF THE PAST
Historical Records of Phenomenal Discoveries

BIGGEST, TALLEST, GREATEST!
Records of Overwhelming Size

BOOK OF ULTIMATE RECORDS

GUINNESS WORLD RECORDS

EXTREME ANIMALS!

Compiled by Kris Hirschmann and Ryan Herndon

For Guinness World Records:
Jennifer Osborne, Laura Barrett Plunkett,
Craig Glenday, Stuart Claxton, Michael Whitty,
and Laura Jackson

SCHOLASTIC INC.
New York Toronto London Auckland Sydney
Mexico City New Delhi Hong Kong Buenos Aires

Attempting to break records or set new records can be dangerous. Appropriate advice should be taken first, and all record attempts are undertaken entirely at the participant's risk. In no circumstances will Guinness World Records Limited or Scholastic Inc. have any liability for death or injury suffered in any record attempts. Guinness World Records Limited has complete discretion over whether or not to include any particular records in the annual *Guinness World Records* book.

Guinness World Records Limited has a very thorough accreditation system for records verification. However, while every effort is made to ensure accuracy, Guinness World Records Limited cannot be held responsible for any errors contained in this work. Feedback from our readers on any point of accuracy is always welcomed.

© 2009 Guinness World Records Limited

No part of this work may be reproduced, stored in a retrieval system, or transmitted in any form or by any means, electronic, mechanical, photocopying, recording, or otherwise, without written permission of the publisher. For information regarding permission, write to Scholastic Inc., Attention: Permissions Department, 557 Broadway, New York, NY 10012.

Published by Scholastic Inc. SCHOLASTIC and associated logos are trademarks and/or registered trademarks of Scholastic Inc.

ISBN-13: 978-0-545-11041-9
ISBN-10: 0-545-11041-6

Designed by Scholastic Art Department
Photo Research by Els Rijper
Records from the Archives of Guinness World Records

12 11 10 9 8 7   11 12 13 14/0

Printed in the U.S.A.

First printing, February 2009

Visit Guinness World Records at www.guinnessworldrecords.com

CONTENTS

The idea for Guinness World Records grew out of a question. In 1951, Sir Hugh Beaver, the managing director of the Guinness Brewery, wanted to know which was the fastest game bird in Europe — the golden plover or the grouse? Some people argued that it was the grouse. Others claimed it was the plover. A book to settle the debate did not exist until Sir Hugh discovered the knowledgeable twin brothers Norris and Ross McWhirter, who lived in London.

Like their father and grandfather, the McWhirter twins loved information. They were kids when they started clipping interesting facts from newspapers and memorizing important dates in world history. As well as learning the names of every river, mountain range, and nation's capital, they knew the record for pole squatting (196 days in 1954), which language had only one irregular verb (Turkish), and that the grouse — flying at a timed speed of 43.5 miles per hour — is faster than the golden plover at 40.4 miles per hour.

Norris and Ross served in the Royal Navy during World War II, graduated from college, and launched their own fact-finding business called McWhirter Twins, Ltd. They were the perfect people to compile the book of records that Sir Hugh Beaver searched for yet could not find.

The first edition of *The Guinness Book of Records* was published on August 27, 1955, and since then has been published in 37 languages and more than 100 countries. In 2000, the book title changed to *Guinness World Records* and has set an incredible record of its own: Excluding non-copyrighted books such as the Bible and the Koran, *Guinness World Records* is the best-selling book of all time!

Today, the official Keeper of the Records keeps a careful eye on each Guinness World Record, compiling and verifying the greatest the world has to offer — from the fastest and the tallest to the slowest and the smallest, with everything in between.

INTRODUCTION

Going Wild!

For more than 50 years, Guinness World Records has measured, weighed, timed, verified, and documented the world's most extreme record-breakers in every category imaginable. Today, the records in their archives number more than 40,000.

In this collection, we'll take a walk on the "wild side" in profiling 46 animals with the most bizarre bodies, odd lifestyles, and unusual talents. We'll chow down with the biggest eaters of the world, from leeches to polar bears. We'll meet a furry fish, fly with a frog, and march alongside the largest ant and crab colonies anywhere.

This book takes you on an extraordinary safari adventure — from night hunting with the aye-aye to scuba diving with the diving bell spider — starring the fastest, furriest, and most ferocious wildlife tracked by Guinness World Records!

CHAPTER 1

Living Among Giants

Scientists have proven that giants aren't mythical beasts. Instead, these enormous creatures dwarf other average-sized species, including human beings! In this chapter, you'll swim with a finned superstar and sunbathe with a gigantic guinea pig. You'll slither alongside a 30-foot snake and check out a 60-foot worm. Here are extremely large monkeys, bugs, lizards, and one monstrous bloodsucker.

Largest Nocturnal Primate

Record Holder:	Aye-aye
Place:	Madagascar

Most of the world's primates are active during daylight hours. The aye-aye (*Daubentonia madagascariensis*) prefers an active nightlife. An endangered species found only on the island of Madagascar, the aye-aye averages between 14 to 16 inches long (not including the tail), and weighs approximately 6 pounds. Although a lightweight when compared to other monkeys, this curious-looking mammal is the **Largest Nocturnal Primate** (pictured). Shy and solitary, aye-ayes spend the day asleep in treetop nests. After sunset, they spend up to 80 percent of the night in search of food.

Drumming Up Dinner

Aye-ayes are omnivorous, able to eat anything from fruit to bugs. They hunt for their favorite food using echolocation, tracking bugs by sound. At night, aye-ayes tap on tree trunks using their long middle fingers. Their enormous ears hear a special "thunk," equal to the ringing of a dinner bell. This sound means insect larvae thrive beneath the tree bark. The aye-ayes use their extra-sized middle finger to dig a hole through the bark and hook a meal.

Madagascar is the fourth largest island of the world. Isolation for millions of years created plants and animal species not found anywhere else on the planet.

Largest Predatory Fish

Record Holder: Great white shark

Place: Oceans worldwide

Get an up-close look at this ferocious fish on this book's front cover.

This finned hunter swims through the tropical and temperate regions of the world's oceans. The great white shark (*Carcharodon carcharias*) has many names: white pointer, white death, and **Largest Predatory Fish**. On average, the great white shark grows 14 to 15 feet in length, with a weight between 1,150 to 1,700 pounds. Some people claim to have seen sharks measuring 33 feet! Think these are fish tales? Evidence suggests that great whites can exceed 20 feet in length. How do they nourish such large bodies? By eating whatever they catch: fish, dolphins, seals, turtles, birds, and whales. Two rows of 3,000 razor-sharp teeth cut up the great white shark's meals for easy (*gulp*) digestion.

Bottom of the List

Encounters with sharks, while rare, are often lethal. However, statistics show that sharks rank much lower than cars as a cause of death in the USA.

Incident	Average annual deaths
Car accidents	44,757
Accidental poisoning	19,456
Drowning	3,306
Bike accidents	742
Sunstroke	273
Collisions with deer	130
Lightning strikes	47
Dog attacks	31
Train crashes	24
Fireworks	11
Shark attacks	1

Largest Lizard

Record Holder:	Komodo dragon
Place:	Indonesia

The **Largest Lizard** isn't *really* a dragon, but it looks like one. Found on the Indonesian islands of Komodo, Rintja, Padar, and Flores, the Komodo dragon (*Varanus komodoensis*) averages 7 feet, 5 inches in length and weighs about 130 pounds. The largest accurately measured specimen was displayed at Missouri's St. Louis Zoological Gardens in 1937. This male weighed 365 pounds with an astonishing length of 10 feet, 2 inches from nose to tail. These gigantic monitor lizards have bacteria-infested mouths. When hunting, the Komodo dragon delivers a quick bite to prey. Then it lets go and stomps off. After a day or two, the lizard returns to its bite victim, now sick or dying from the infected wound. The weakened animals are easy pickings for the hungry dragon.

Longest Snake

Record Holder:	Reticulated python
Place:	Indonesia, Southeast Asia, and the Philippines

The **Longest Snake** may be long enough to stretch up your bedroom wall, across the ceiling, and down the opposite wall. The reticulated python (*Python reticulatus*) lives in Indonesia, Southeast Asia, and the Philippines. These slithering reptiles usually reach adult lengths of 20 to 23 feet (pictured). Sometimes they grow bigger — *much* bigger. In 1912, one specimen in Celebes, Indonesia, measured 32 feet, 9 inches long. Large snakes are capable of eating huge meals. A reticulated python wraps its muscular coils around prey and squeezes until the prey suffocates. The python then swallows its meal headfirst! Pythons can unhinge their jaws when consuming prey larger than their own heads. Flexible belly skin stretches to make room for meals as large as pigs and . . . people!

RECORD 5

Largest Rodent

Record Holder:	Capybara
Place:	Central and South America

Deep in the wetlands of Central and South America lives an enormous rodent! Measuring about 4 feet from nose to rump and weighing up to 174 pounds, the capybara or carpincho (*Hydrochoerus hydrochaeris*) is the **Largest Rodent** on the planet alive today. Two to four million years ago, the now-extinct rodent named *Josephoartigasia monesi* was the size of a bear at 10 feet long and 2,200 pounds! The capybara resembles a giant guinea pig. Shy and gentle, it spends the morning and evening hours munching on grass and plants. It rests on riverbanks during the hottest part of the day, trotting into the river for a refreshing dip (pictured).

Largest Parasites

Record Holder:	Broad or fish tapeworm
Place:	Worldwide

EXTREME FACTS

Adult tapeworms lay up to 1 million eggs per day. These eggs pass out of the host's body along with waste products. If they find their way into water or food, they may be consumed by a new host. The eggs will hatch inside the body. If conditions are good, they will grow up to be just like their parasitic parents.

A worm the length of a school bus could be living inside your body *right now*. The broad or fish tapeworm (*Diphyllobothrium latum*) is a parasite that mainly infests fish but sometimes wriggles its way through the human body. Measuring up to 60 feet from end to end, these colossal invertebrates are by far the **Largest Parasites** on Earth. They rest comfortably in the folds of the small intestine, feeding on the host's partially digested food. A tapeworm spends up to 20 years feasting before dying and breaking into fleshy chunks, which are expelled one by one from the host's body.

Largest Leech

Record Holder:	Giant Amazon leech
Place:	South America

Not every animal eats solid food to stay alive. A leech is a freshwater worm parasite that survives by drinking the blood of other creatures (pictured). The **Largest Leech** is the giant Amazon leech (*Haementaria ghilianii*) found in the rain forests of South America. It measures a whopping 18 inches from head to tail. That's four or five times longer than most leech species! This monstrous bloodsucker suctions itself to victims with its mouthparts. A 6-inch-long retractable tongue called a proboscis pierces the victim's skin and, using it like a straw, the leech draws blood into its own body.

Do vampires exist? Keep your eyes open while hunting for the different species of blood-drinkers profiled in this book.

Doctor Leech, M.D.

Would you run away if you saw a leech in your doctor's office? Not always! Biotherapy is the use of living organisms in medical diagnosis and treatment. The use of leeches to reduce swelling and increase blood flow in surgical patients dates back to the Egyptians. How does leech attachment work medically? A doctor attaches the leech to the patient's damaged body parts. While the leech gets a meal, it also helps the patient by injecting natural blood thinners and breaking down blood clots. Wounds heal quicker and cleaner than they would without the leeches' aid.

EXTREME FACTS

A numbing ingredient in the saliva makes the leech's bite almost painless. Another ingredient called an anticoagulant prevents blood from clotting while the leech feeds. Many victims don't know they have been bitten until after a leech has finished its meal and slunk off into the darkness.

Longest Insect

Record Holder:	Stick insect
Place:	Malaysia

Stick insects are masters of camouflage, able to hide in plain sight by blending into their environment. Find the stick insect disguised as a tree branch in this book's color photo section.

There are more than 2,000 different species of stick insects in the world. These bugs are unusually large, so how do they protect themselves from hungry predators? Some species' blood is toxic, tastes terrible, and is the best defense. That's if a predator can even *find* a stick insect to catch. These gigantic bugs have long, thin, knobby bodies that look exactly like . . . the tree branches they live on! The **Longest Insect** in overall length is the *Phobaeticus serratipes* stick insect of Malaysia. Its body is 11 inches long. But when it stretches out its legs, its total length increases to a record-setting 21 inches!

Heaviest Scorpion

Record Holder:	Emperor scorpion
Place:	West Africa

The scaly armor of the scorpion species reflects ultraviolet (UV) light. See how the scorpion "glows" in this book's special color photo section.

Measuring between 5 and 7 inches in length, the emperor scorpion (*Pandinus imperator*) of West Africa isn't the biggest member of the scorpion family. But it takes the prize at weigh-in time. This thick-bodied arachnid is the world's **Heaviest Scorpion**, tipping the scales at about 2 ounces. That's the weight of a jumbo-size chicken egg! The emperor scorpion uses its bulk to catch and kill prey, including termites, cockroaches, and even the occasional mouse. It defends itself from other predators by stinging with its barbed tail or delivering a painful pinch with its powerful, jagged claws.

That's a Mouthful!

People interact with nature every day, but some people get a little too close for comfort. The emperor scorpion's sting is venomous, with a claw pinch powerful enough to snap a pencil in half. But scary facts didn't stop Dean Sheldon of the USA from opening up and saying "Aaaah" for this miniature monster. In August 2006, Dean placed a 7-inch-long emperor scorpion in his mouth and held it there for a full 18 seconds (pictured). Whatever Dean's secret weapon is, he emerged from his Guinness World Record attempt with his tongue intact — and the record for **Largest Scorpion Held in the Mouth** as his reward.

EXTREME FACTS

Emperor scorpions give birth to live young. There are about 12 babies, called "scorplings," in a brood. The scorplings ride on their mother's back until they are several months old. As they grow, they leave this "nest" for short trips out into the bigger world to hunt and explore.

CHAPTER 2

Natural Talents

All animals have interesting features and abilities. But "interesting" isn't enough to earn a Guinness World Record. Every record-holder must meet strict criteria, even if the contender is a shrimp! In this chapter, you'll meet a squid that can light up a dark room, a frog smelly enough to clear that same room, and a shrimp able to punch through solid glass. In nature's talent show, these champions win top honors!

Fish with the Greatest Sense of Smell

Record Holder:	Shark
Place:	Oceans worldwide

EXTREME FACTS

Besides their super sense of smell, sharks have other incredible abilities that aid in locating a satisfying meal. A sensory system named the lateral line detects distant vibrations, such as those made by struggling fish. Sharks also have electrosensors that pick up on the weak electrical currents given off by all living creatures.

It's a big ocean out there. How does a predator find food in the water? If you're a shark, you sniff it out! As the **Fish with the Greatest Sense of Smell**, sharks of all species have more highly developed scent organs than any other fish. Scientists believe that about two-thirds of the shark's *entire brain* is devoted to the sense of smell. With so much processing power, a shark can detect one part of blood in 100 million parts of water. Sharks are the bloodhounds of the sea.

Smelliest Frog

Record Holder:	Venezuelan skunk frog
Place:	Venezuela

Unknown to science until 1991, the Venezuelan skunk frog (*Aromobates nocturnus*) is the largest member of the poison-arrow frog family, Dendrobatidae. Instead of poisonous skin like its cousin has, this frog's secret weapon is its distinctive and record-setting odor. Measuring only 2.44 inches in length, the skunk frog is smaller than the mammal it is named after — but its stink is just as strong! Like its namesake, the skunk frog releases foul-smelling chemicals through its skin when threatened. The stench is (*cough*) unpleasant enough to put any predator off its plan to dine upon the **Smelliest Frog**.

You-Reeka!

The smelly Venezuelan skunk frog wouldn't stop Madeline Albrecht, the world's most experienced reek detector. Madeline worked for 15 years quality-checking the odor-reducing products created by Hill Top Research Laboratories in Cincinnati, Ohio. After an estimated 5,600 feet and thousands of armpits nose-proofed by the year 2000, Madeline earned the title for **Most Feet and Armpits Sniffed**. Maybe she could recommend the perfect deodorant for this stinky amphibian.

Farthest Gliding Amphibian

Record Holder:	Costa Rican flying frog
Place:	Costa Rica

Flip to this book's special color photo section for a glimpse of the gloriously green Costa Rican flying frog in full flight.

Look, up in the sky! It's a bird . . . it's a plane . . . no, it's a . . . frog? The Costa Rican flying frog (*Agalychnis spurrelli*) is the **Farthest Gliding Amphibian**. This small yet powerful jumper can glide up to 50 feet through the air. To glide between places, the flying frog extends its arms and legs and spreads its toes wide. Webs of skin between the toes catch the air and act like natural parachutes to slow the frog's descent. These frogs fly between tree branches, laying their eggs on leaves hanging above pools of water. Four days later, tadpoles emerge from the eggs and spill into the water below like rain from the sky.

Noisiest Land Animal

Record Holder:	Howler monkey
Place:	Central and South America

At dawn and dusk, the rainforests of Central and South America echo with the shrieks and screams of the **Noisiest Land Animal** (pictured). The calls of the howler monkey (*Alouatta*) would make the perfect alarm system. A male howler in full voice can be heard clearly up to 3 miles away. The sound has been described as a mix of a dog's bark and a donkey's bray — magnified many times. How does a howler monkey howl? A large voice box combined with an odd-shaped, hollow bone named the hyoid amplifies sound, acting like built-in stereo speakers. Howler monkeys use their high-volume voices to advertise their position and warn other monkeys to stay out of their territory.

Most Fearless Mammal

Record Holder:	Ratel or honey badger
Place:	Africa and Asia

Don't badger the ratel (pictured). Also known as the honey badger (*Mellivora capensis*), the ratel is the **Most Fearless Mammal**. It's not about size. Ratels are fairly small at 24 to 30 inches long and weighing 29 pounds or less. It's about fierceness in a fight. Found in the forests and savannas of Africa, the Middle East, India, and Nepal, the ratel is hunted by hyenas and leopards. But the ratel has a few tricks up its . . . skin. Tough and loose are the secrets of the ratel's pelt. Bee stings, porcupine quills, and snakebites can't penetrate the ratel's tough hide. And the pelt is loose, preventing larger predators from getting a solid grip on the ratel. If snagged, the ratel twists around inside its loose suit of skin and bites the attacker back until one of them — usually the bigger guy — lets go and runs away.

Strongest Animal Punch

Record Holder: Peacock mantis shrimp

Place: Indian and Pacific Oceans

Swim over to this book's special color photo section for a safe view of this feisty fighter.

EXTREME FACTS

The peacock mantis shrimp is a dual Guinness World Record-holder! This stomatopod also boasts the **Most Sophisticated Eyes**. While humans perceive a range of three visual pigments (blue, green, red) through our retina's cone cells, the peacock mantis shrimp's eyes can perceive more than 10 different visual pigments. If that wasn't impressive enough, eight different eyecup muscles operate the crustacean's two mobile eyestalks, allowing a single eye to track movement in the opposite direction up to 70 degrees apart.

The peacock mantis shrimp (*Odontodactylus scyllarus*) isn't a peacock, a mantis, or even a shrimp. It's a colorful marine crustacean known as a stomatopod. If you ever see one while snorkeling, don't touch it because it might knock you out! The 12-inch-long peacock mantis shrimp can flail its club-shaped front legs outward at speeds of 75 feet per second, delivering a blow strong enough to shatter the shells of prey or even to break aquarium glass. The force of the blow is over a hundred times greater than the creature's own weight, making it the **Strongest Animal Punch** anywhere on land or sea.

Record Holder:	Firefly squid
Place:	Japan

See the bright lights on the firefly squid's body in this book's special color photo section.

It would take about a thousand lightning bugs to equal the glow of one *Watasenia scintillans*, the world's **Most Bioluminescent Squid**. Commonly called the firefly squid, this organism lives in deep waters off the coast of northern Japan. Its days are spent far below the water's surface. At night, it rises to the surface and feeds in a truly flashy style! The firefly squid's 2.5-inch body is covered with glowing dots that blink on and off in complicated patterns. Scientists believe the squid uses this light show to communicate with other squids, to disguise its shape, and to confuse predators.

The firefly squid's light-producing organs are called photophores. Thousands of tiny photophores cover every part of the squid's body. Larger photophores are found on the tentacle tips and around the squid's eyes. These organs give off a deep blue glow, lighting up the water wherever firefly squids make their homes.

Shining Seas

From March to May every year, millions and, at times, billions of firefly squid gather in Japan's Tomoya Bay. The squid flash and glitter while laying eggs in one of the world's most incredible mass-spawning events. After the eggs are fertilized, the squid die and sink to the ocean floor or wash onto the beach, where a miles-long pileup of glowing corpses forms. People come from all over the world to witness this event, not seen anywhere else.

CHAPTER 3

Eaters and Speedsters

Two key skills are critical for survival. First, you must keep yourself well fed. Second, you must be faster than anything that wants to eat you! In this chapter, you'll dine with bloodthirsty birds, toothy fish, and a mole able to clean its plate in record time before dashing off to avoid speedy snakes. From diet talk to fast walks, it's a feast of information . . . and you're invited!

Greatest Eater Relative to Weight

Record Holder: North American silk moth caterpillar

Place: USA and Canada

EXTREME FACTS

Newborn human babies weigh about 7 pounds. If a baby of this size were to match the North American silk moth caterpillar's dietary habits, it would have to eat 601,800 pounds of food before turning two months old.

Talk about an appetite! Eating up to 86,000 times its own weight during its first 56 days of life, the caterpillar of the North American silk moth (*Antheraea polyphemus*) is the **Greatest Eater Relative to Weight**. Found in most parts of the USA and Canada, these insects hatch in April and begin eating, starting with their own eggshell. The eating frenzy ends when it's cocoon-spinning time. All is quiet while the caterpillar transforms into an adult moth. Once it emerges, the moth takes wing to lay eggs for a new generation — and the cycle begins again with more hungry caterpillars.

Most Bloodthirsty Bird

Record Holder:	Sharp-beaked ground finch
Place:	Galapagos Islands

Yikes!
First leeches, now bloodsucking birds! Keep hunting for the last vampire of an entirely different species.

EXTREME FACTS

Water is crucial for survival. Sources of fresh water are scarce on Wolf Island. Scientists believe this limitation is why the vampire finch resorts to drinking blood.

Found throughout the Galapagos Islands, most sharp-beaked ground finches (*Geospiza difficilis*) feed on seeds and insects. But the finches that live in one region known as Wolf Island prefer a liquid refreshment . . . blood! These tiny birds fly up to a larger type of seabird and peck at them, pretending to be helpful by removing parasites. Meanwhile, the finches are gouging holes into the bigger bird's skin and drinking their unsuspecting victim's blood. This gruesome habit earned these thirsty birds the Guinness World Record for **Most Bloodthirsty Bird** and a nightmarish nickname, "vampire finch."

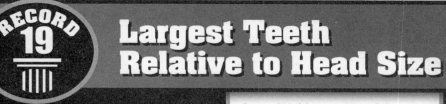
Record Holder:	Viperfish
Place:	Tropical and temperate seas worldwide

Eating is tricky when your teeth are too big to fit inside your mouth. But the deep-sea viperfish (*Chauliodus sloani*), record-holder for the **Largest Teeth Relative to Head Size**, accomplishes this delicate task (pictured). The viperfish opens its mouth wide, making its jaws completely vertical. Then it lunges. Small fish are impaled on the viperfish's 0.4-inch-tall, needlelike teeth, equal to half the width of the viperfish's head. The speared prey is sucked into the viperfish's 11-inch body, where it provides energy for the toothy terror's attacks. Viperfish are vertical migrators. They move up and down the water column depending on time of day. During sunlit hours, viperfish hunt at depths down to 8,200 feet. At nightfall, viperfish rise into the shallower waters above 2,000 feet.

Animal with the Largest Prey

Record Holder: Polar bear
Place: The Arctic

The polar bear is the **Largest Land Carnivore** at 8 feet, 6 inches from nose to tail, and weighing up to 1,320 pounds. Those measurements are *before* a whale-sized dinner.

In the frozen Arctic, food is scarce and only the toughest survive. This difficult habitat is home to the polar bear (*Ursus maritimus*), the world's largest and hungriest bear species (pictured). To get the nutrition their enormous bodies require, polar bears hunt the biggest game around: walruses and beluga whales weighing more than 1,000 pounds. As the record-holder for **Animal with the Largest Prey**, the polar bear repeatedly proves that it is more than up for the challenge.

The polar bear's nose really does help it fill its enormous stomach! Equipped with the **Most Sensitive Nose of All Land Mammals**, polar bears can sniff out a seal meal up to 18 miles away and under a thick sheet of ice.

EXTREME FACTS

An adult male polar bear can fit about 150 pounds of meat into its stomach. It prefers seals but will attack any animal if hungry enough. This extreme hunting behavior is most common during summertime, when the Arctic ice pack shrinks and reduces the polar bear's hunting grounds.

Fastest Eater (Mammals)

Record Holder: Star-nosed mole
Place: North America

Stare into the mouth of the star-nosed mole in this book's special color photo section.

EXTREME FACTS

Although star-nosed moles breathe air, they can also smell underwater! They blow bubbles onto underwater objects. After a short time, they snort the bubbles back into their noses and "read" any scent picked up.

In an animal-eating race, the star-nosed mole (*Condylura cristata*) of Canada and the northeastern USA would capture the blue ribbon! According to research published by Dr. Kenneth Catania, this mammal with the star-shaped nose averages just 230 milliseconds — less than one-quarter of a second — in using its hand-like snout to identify, capture, consume, and move on to the next meal. If the mole is in a rush, the **Fastest Eater (Mammals)** speeds up the process to 120 milliseconds. And your family thought *you* gobbled down your food too fast!

Fastest-Running Flying Bird

Record Holder:	North American roadrunner
Place:	Southwestern USA

EXTREME FACTS

Roadrunners also use their running skills for hunting. These birds forage on the ground for food, catching insects, lizards, rodents, snakes, tarantulas, and smaller birds.

Would you run if you could fly? Maybe the North American roadrunner (*Geococcyx californianus*) forgot that it is the **Fastest-Running Flying Bird** (pictured). Found in the southwestern USA, this larger member of the ground cuckoo family measures about 22 inches long and likes to keep its feet on the ground. It uses its long legs and strong toes to outrun predators, capable of reaching up to 26 miles per hour. When faced with a swifter predator, the roadrunner will take to the air. But mostly, this bird prefers to sprint rather than soar.

Fastest Dive

Record Holder:	Peregrine falcon
Place:	Worldwide

In freefall, a human skydiver travels at a top speed of about 120 miles per hour. That's *waaaay* slower than the dive of the peregrine falcon (*Falco peregrinus*), which can zoom down at 186 miles per hour (pictured)! This ballistic bird soars at high altitudes, looking for smaller fowl flying far below. When it spots a meal, the peregrine falcon folds back its tail and wings, tucks in its feet, and goes into the world's **Fastest Dive**. The falcon uses its speed as a weapon, knocking its prey senseless before plucking it out of midair and enjoying a leisurely snack.

Back from the Brink

Captive peregrine falcons are sometimes used to scare other birds away from airport runways.

In the 1970s, peregrine falcons became endangered because of the use of pesticides by human beings. The pesticides did not kill the birds outright. They built up in the falcons' tissues, causing chemical changes that made the birds' eggshells fragile. Most of the eggs broke before the chicks inside could develop. This led to a plunge in worldwide peregrine populations. Today, however, the worst pesticides have been banned, and peregrine falcons are making an impressive comeback. In the USA, these birds were removed from the endangered species list in 1999.

Fastest Snake on Land

Record Holder: Black mamba
Place: Africa

EXTREME FACTS

One bite by the black mamba contains 10 times the amount of venom capable of killing an adult human. This venom paralyzes the muscles used for respiration. Unable to breathe, the mamba's victims quickly suffocate. Nearly 100 percent of people bitten by a black mamba die within 20 minutes if immediate medical treatment is not received.

Only a fast runner could outpace the **Fastest Snake on Land**. The black mamba (*Dendroaspis polytepis*) of tropical Africa has been clocked at speeds up to 12 miles per hour for short distances across flat ground. The speed is impressive considering the sheer size of this scary snake. From tip to tail, black mambas can grow up to 14 feet long. Normally shy and preferring flight to fights, this grayish snake is an aggressive fighter if cornered. Its name comes from the black color of the inside of its mouth, the last thing a victim sees. A black mamba about to strike raises one-third of its body off the ground, gives several warning hisses, and — if you haven't started running away — attacks multiple times.

Terrifying Tails

Like black mambas, rattlesnakes are highly venomous. But this fact doesn't bother "Snakeman" Jackie Bibby, who holds multiple Guinness World Records for handling rattlesnakes in jaw-dropping ways (pictured). On November 9, 2006, this fearless American broke his most famous reptilian record for **Most Live Rattlesnakes Held in Mouth.** Jackie held 10 live rattlesnakes in his mouth by their tails, without any assistance, for 10 seconds during Guinness World Records Day in New York City, New York, USA.

CHAPTER 4

Bizarre Bodies

Hair on a frog . . . built-in spears on a whale . . . and six eyes on a fish? Mother Nature has a vivid imagination, and weird-looking wildlife is the result. This chapter spotlights record-holders with exaggerated features, from long noses to large claws. There's even an animal that makes scientists scratch their heads because they're stumped in classifying it. Hop aboard and enjoy a strange and wooly ride!

Fish with the Most Eyes

Record Holder:	Six-eyed spookfish
Place:	Northeastern Pacific Ocean

EXTREME FACTS

What's up with all those eyes? Scientists hypothesize the six-eyed spookfish uses its extra eyeballs to collect as much light as possible in the dim ocean depths. Plus, those eyes point in different directions, providing a greater range of vision to spot approaching danger . . . or curious photographers!

On the inky-black ocean floor, many creatures don't have any eyes. They use other senses to "see." The six-eyed spookfish (*Bathylychnops exilis*) went to the opposite extreme. Living at depths of 300 to 3,000 feet in the north-eastern Pacific Ocean, this fish has not two, not four, but SIX eyes. That's enough eyeballs to "watch over" the title of **Fish with the Most Eyes**. More oddly, the second and third pairs of eyes are located *inside* the principal eyes. The second pair is positioned within the lower half of the main eyeballs. The third pair nestles behind the second-ary globes, where it reflects light into the main eyes.

Longest Whale Tooth

Record Holder: Narwhal
Place: Arctic Ocean

How would you feel about spending your entire life with a huge pole sticking out of your face? If you were a narwhal (*Monodon monoceros*), you'd probably like it just fine! Found in the Atlantic and Russian areas of the Arctic Ocean, these marine mammals grow long, spiraled ivory tusks from their mouths (pictured). The tusks average 6 feet, 6 inches in length, but can grow nearly 10 feet long in larger individuals. One tusk can weigh up to 22 pounds and have a maximum girth of about 9 inches. That's the world's **Longest Whale Tooth**, and also one of the largest natural spears on *any* animal. *En garde!*

Unicorns of the Sea

Hundreds of years ago, people sometimes found narwhal tusks washed up on beaches. They thought these objects were the horns of the legendary unicorn. Since unicorns were magical creatures, the "horns" were believed to contain special powers. Narwhal tusks became sought-after treasures, worth several times their weight in gold. During the 16th century, Queen Elizabeth of England received a carved, bejeweled narwhal tusk worth an estimated 10,000 pounds — enough money, at the time, to build an entire castle.

EXTREME FACTS

All male narwhals grow tusks. Females usually do not, although a few tusked females have been found. Occasionally, a narwhal grows two tusks instead of the usual single tooth. Scientists estimate that about one out of every 500 males is double-tusked.

Largest Eye-to-Body Ratio

Record Holder:	Vampire squid
Place:	Tropical oceans

Hiding in the shadowy sea, the vampire squid is rarely photographed. But the Monterey Bay Aquarium Research Institute sent an up-close snapshot for this book's special color photo section.

The vampire squid (*Vampyroteuthis infernalis*) lives at ocean depths of more than 1,970 feet. In this lightless part of the sea, many animals have the natural ability to glow. This trait is called bioluminescence. We've already met an example in the firefly squid (Record 16). Equipped with super-sized eyes, the vampire squid can see every underwater creature's special shine! This creature has a maximum body length of only 11 inches, but eyes that measure 0.9 inches across. That's a ratio of 1:11, which is the **Largest Eye-to-Body Ratio** in the animal kingdom. A human would need eyes the size of table-tennis paddles — and a MUCH larger head to hold them — to compete with the vampire squid's phenomenal peepers.

SHOWING BIZARRE FACES . . .

© Fletcher and Baylis/
Photo Researchers, Inc.

GUINNESS WORLD RECORDS TM

THE NOSE KNOWS
Can the proboscis monkey see beyond its nose? Having the **Longest Primate Nose** makes it easy to identify this monkey among its many cousins. Check out the incredible variety of fur, teeth, eyes, and claws on display in "Bizarre Bodies."

AND FOUND IN EXOTIC PLACES

© Dante Fenolio/
Photo Researchers, Inc.

FLYING CIRCUS
Like the famous flying-circus elephant it is named after, the dumbo octopus uses its large earlike fins to maneuver up and down in the ocean. Visit the habitat of the **Deepest Octopus** and others in "Lifestyles of the Wild and Free."

THESE EXTREME ANIMALS

Kim Reisenbichler © 1996 MBARI

LIVING FOSSIL
The scientists at the Monterey Bay Aquarium Research Institute (**MBARI**) use robot submarines to study the vampire squid in its natural deep-sea habitat. Learn more about this record-holder of **Largest Eye-to-Body Ratio** in "Bizarre Bodies."

GLOW BRIGHTER

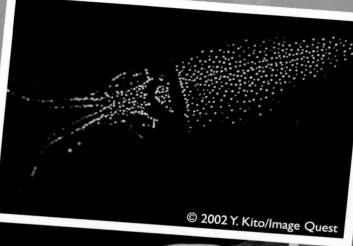

© 2002 Y. Kito/Image Quest

© Paul and Joyce Berquist/
Animals Animals

NIGHT LIGHTS

Some animals glow in various types of light. The firefly squid as **Most Bioluminescent Squid** scares off predators with its shining body. The **Most Dangerous Glowing Animal** is the scorpion species with its ultraviolet-reflective armor. Heed wildlife's warnings in "Natural Talents" and "Cautionary Tales."

ESCAPE QUICKER

© Michael and Patricia Fogden/Corbis

© Premaphotos/
Nature Picture Library

FLY OR HIDE

The Costa Rican flying frog's jumping talent makes escape easy for the **Farthest Gliding Amphibian.** Many stick insect species are record-holders for extreme body length. Natural coloring helps these big bugs hide in plain sight. Discover more animal abilities in "Natural Talents" and "Living Among Giants."

GUINNESS WORLD RECORDS TM

EAT FASTER

© Gary Meszaros/Photo Researchers, Inc.

DIG IT
The star-nosed mole's sensitive snout locates food. After its paddle-shaped paws clear a path, the **Fastest Eater (Mammals)** dines on tasty worms and bugs. Take a break with "Eaters and Speedsters" for more dietary and racing records.

STOP THE SHOW

© Frank Greenaway/
Dorling Kindersley/
Getty Images

IN-FLIGHT AIR BRAKES
Think the peacock has impressive plumage?
Fly with Reeves's pheasant, record-holder for
Longest Feathers in a Wild Bird Species.
This bird uses its tail to stop in mid-air. Spend a day
with amazing species in "Lifestyles of the Wild and Free."

KNOCK OUT ANY CHALLENGER

© SeaPics.com

THE CHAMPION

Small doesn't mean weak. The **Strongest Animal Punch** clocks in at 100 times the body weight of the peacock mantis shrimp when shattering the shells of its prey. Meet more unusual record-breakers in "Natural Talents."

.... TO BE A GUINNESS WORLD RECORD-HOLDER!

Longest Primate Nose

Record Holder: Proboscis monkey
Place: Borneo

See the proboscis monkey's unusual face in this book's special color photo section.

EXTREME FACTS

In addition to their large noses, proboscis monkeys have big bellies. Their huge stomachs can store up to one-quarter of the monkey's weight in food! This built-in storage tank allows the proboscis monkey to spend most of its time in trees, where leaves are its main food source.

The word "proboscis" means "nose," and it's no wonder the proboscis monkey (*Nasalis larvatus*) of Borneo was named for its distinctive feature. Males of this species have droopy noses that can be up to 7 inches long. That's the world's **Longest Primate Nose**! Often large enough to hang over the mouth, this appendage gets red and swollen when its owner is afraid or excited. In this state, the bulging nose acts like an amplifier to increase the volume of the monkey's calls. Now that's what you call a *real* honker!

Largest Claws on a Living Animal

Record Holder: Giant armadillo
Place: South America

Lions and tigers and bears have claws, oh my! But none can compete with the giant armadillo (*Priodontes maximus*), which sports the **Largest Claws on a Living Animal** (pictured). The forefeet of the armadillo are curved talons measuring 8 inches in length. Those are some mighty sharp weapons for a 3-foot-long animal that likes to keep to itself. The armadillo puts these nails to the test daily. Its record-breaking claws dig burrows in the ground and tear apart the termite mounds that dot its South American home range. A giant armadillo weighs between 40 to 70 pounds on average, with some individuals reaching 130 pounds! Their appetite matches their body size. These animals can consume the entire population of a termite mound. They also have been known to dine upon larger prey, including rats, tapirs, and carrion in their role as nature's pest-controller.

The famous body armor worn by all armadillo species is made up of 14 to 17 flexible bands of horn and bone. A helmet-shaped extension covers the head while smaller, tightly packed plates sheath the tail.

Nature's Pest Control Service

When people have a termite or ant infestation in their homes, they call a pest-control service. Mother Nature created the giant armadillo. Instead of bait traps or poisonous sprays, this amazing animal uses its record-setting teeth to eat away at the problem. Besides having the **Largest Claws on a Living Animal**, the giant armadillo is also the **Land Mammal with the Most Teeth.** Approximately 100 teeth line the inside of this mammal's long snout, perfect for grinding up ants and termites. Unfortunately, crop farmers consider the giant armadillo a pest because of its ability to tunnel underground and disrupt the growing crop roots.

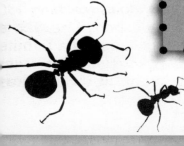

Most Unclassifiable Mammal

Record Holder:	Aardvark
Place:	Africa

EXTREME FACTS

Most of the aardvark's diet consists of ants and termites. The aardvark finds these insects at home. But there's no polite knock on the front door. The aardvark rips apart insect nests with its strong front legs. After devouring an entire colony of ants, the aardvark settles down for an after-dinner nap in the ants' hollowed-out nest.

This animal is a guessing game for anyone curious about solving the mystery of its heritage. It is distantly related to shrews, manatees, and elephants. It looks a lot like an ant-eater and sort of like a pig (its name means "earth pig"). But the aardvark (*Orycteropus afer*), which is found only in Africa, fits into none of these groups (pictured). This creature is incredibly peculiar anatomically — so peculiar, in fact, that it cannot be classified with any other living species of mammal. Scientists have been forced to give this odd-bodied animal an entire order of its own, Tubulidentata or "tube teeth." That means the aardvark, as the world's **Most Unclassifiable Mammal**, is literally in a class of its own!

Many other animals move into the aardvark's home after the original owner moves out. Birds, porcupines, warthogs, hares, and monitor lizards are just a few of the animals that curl up inside the aardvark's empty burrow.

Furriest Frog

Record Holder:	Hairy frog
Place:	West Africa

EXTREME FACTS

Female hairy frogs lay their eggs in fast-flowing rivers. Males protect the eggs from predators until hatching time. Thanks to their hairy, breathing legs, the males can stay underwater for days without surfacing for air.

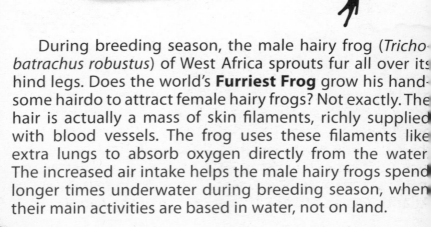

During breeding season, the male hairy frog (*Trichobatrachus robustus*) of West Africa sprouts fur all over its hind legs. Does the world's **Furriest Frog** grow his handsome hairdo to attract female hairy frogs? Not exactly. The hair is actually a mass of skin filaments, richly supplied with blood vessels. The frog uses these filaments like extra lungs to absorb oxygen directly from the water. The increased air intake helps the male hairy frogs spend longer times underwater during breeding season, when their main activities are based in water, not on land.

Furriest Fish

The name *Mirapinna esau* means "hairy with wonderful fins." It's clear how the fish earned the "hairy" part of this name. The "wonderful fins" part comes from the fish's uniquely lobed pelvic fins, which are huge and stick out of both sides of the body. In addition to these features, *Mirapinna esau* has an unusual humped back that would make this fish easy to identify — if the fur wasn't already a dead giveaway, that is!

Record Holder: *Mirapinna esau*
Place: Atlantic Ocean

Most fish are covered with scales. Maybe that style wasn't fancy enough for *Mirapinna esau*. This strange ocean dweller is covered with fur instead! The "fur" isn't actually hair. It's a thick mass of living body growths. No one knows what these growths do — other than to earn the Guinness World Record for **Furriest Fish**! Measuring just 2.5 inches in length, *Mirapinna esau* was discovered in 1911, after a specimen was caught in the middle of the Atlantic Ocean about 547 miles north of the Azores.

The Winner, by a Hair

When it comes to fur, the Ramos Gomez family of Mexico more than gives the hairiest fish and frog a run for their money. The 19 members of this five-generation clan suffer from a condition called congenital generalized hypertrichosis that causes excessive hair growth. The women of the family are covered with a light to medium coat of hair. The men have thick hair on about 98 percent of their bodies, excluding only the hands and feet. Time for a haircut? Nope! The Ramos Gomezes are happy to be the **Hairiest Family** in the world. "I'd never cut the hair off," says Victor "Larry" Ramos Gomez (pictured). "I'm very proud to be who I am."

CHAPTER 5

Cautionary Tales

DANGER! You're about to meet some of nature's deadliest creatures. This chapter is chock-full of animals you don't want to mess with, including a glow-in-the-dark arachnid, a bird with poisonous feathers, a car-length killer snake, and a seal that would just love to have you for dinner. Speaking of dinner, how would you like to try a popular seafood dish that could kill you if the chef cuts left instead of right? It's time to explore a world where Guinness World Record-breaking danger lurks around every corner!

Record Holder: Piranha

Place: South America

If you want to keep your toes intact, don't dip them into some rivers in South America. These waters are home to the notorious piranha, which has a well-deserved reputation as the world's **Most Ferocious Freshwater Fish**. Most piranhas are between 6 and 10 inches long. They are easily recognized by their jagged teeth, which grow in rows on both the top and bottom jaws (pictured). About 20 fish make up a school. Piranhas of the generas *Serrasalmus* and *Pygocentrus* are especially dangerous. When a wounded or sick animal enters the river, its blood and splashing soon attracts the school's attention. The school works together to strip the flesh off creatures as large as horses within minutes, leaving nothing but a skeleton behind.

A Bad Rep

There's no doubt that piranhas can be nasty and aggressive toward other animals. But have they truly earned their killer reputation when humans are involved? Piranhas have nipped swimmers, but these attacks are more of a nuisance than anything serious. The school prefers easier prey, such as smaller fish or even seeds. Yes, that's right… piranhas can be vegetarians, but this fish prefers an eat-all-you-see diet. Take note of this cautionary tale from September 19, 1981. An overloaded boat capsized during docking procedures at the port of Obidos, Brazil. More than 300 passengers reportedly fell overboard, where they were killed and eaten by piranha.

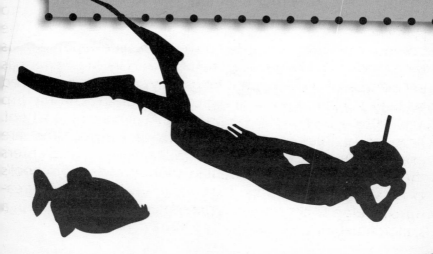

Most Poisonous Edible Fish

Record Holder:	Puffer fish
Place:	Red Sea and Indo-Pacific region

EXTREME FACTS

In Japan, only specially licensed chefs are allowed to prepare *fugu-sashi*. To earn this license, they must take a written test and a fish-identification test. Then they must prepare an actual puffer fish and eat it themselves. Only 30 percent of the applicants pass this rigorous test. The other 70 percent we hope pursue a different career . . . or maybe they never finish cleaning their plate? *Gulp!*

Found in the Red Sea and the Indo-Pacific region, members of the puffer fish (*Tetraodon*) family are among the world's most poisonous creatures. The ovaries, eggs, blood, skin, liver, and intestines of this fish contain a powerful poison called tetrodotoxin. It takes less than 0.004 ounce of this poison to kill a human being. Despite this dangerous side effect, the flesh of the puffer fish is considered a delicacy in Japan. Called *fugu-sashi* (blowfish-raw), this dish is perfectly safe if prepared properly — and fatal within 20 minutes if not. Diners take a life-or-death gamble every time they eat a piece of the **Most Poisonous Edible Fish**.

Most Dangerous Pinniped

Record Holder:	Leopard seal
Place:	Antarctica and far southern coasts

A pinniped is a meat-eating, flippered marine animal. The world's **Most Dangerous Pinniped** is the bad-tempered, 10-foot long, 750-pound leopard seal (*Hydrurga leptonyx*). Found in Antarctica and along the world's far southern coasts, leopard seals are named after its spotted neck area. These carnivores fill their bellies with fish and squid, but also enjoy a penguin meal (pictured). This fact might explain why leopard seals are the only pinniped known to attack people for no identifiable reason. Scientists think leopard seals confuse the dark vertical shapes of people with those of the almost-human-height emperor penguins. Leopard seals have reportedly lunged through cracks in the ice to snap at people's feet, attacked divers, and chased people across the ice for distances of up to 330 feet!

Most Poisonous Bird

Record Holder:	Hooded pitohui
Place:	Papua New Guinea

EXTREME FACTS

The hooded pitohui was discovered in 1990. The bird's poisonous secretions puzzled scientists until recently, when researchers found a common link between the diets of the poisonous bird and an amphibian: a toxic bug! The Choresine beetle (family Melyridae) exists in both species' habitats and might prove to be the source of the batrachotoxins found in the hooded pitohui and the unrelated but deadlier dart frog.

The word "pitohui" sounds like something you might say when spitting out a bad-tasting morsel. It is therefore the perfect name for the world's **Most Poisonous Bird**! The feathers and skin of the hooded pitohui (*Pitohui dichrous*) of Papua New Guinea are coated with a powerful poison called homobatrachotoxin. That's the same nasty stuff found on the dart frogs of South America. It can make attackers sick or even kill them. Predators therefore stay far away from this bird, which advertises its deadly nature with a bad smell and bright colors.

Longest Venomous Snake

Record Holder:	King cobra
Place:	Southeast Asia and India

The head of a king cobra is as big as a man's hand. In one bite, the king cobra's fearsome fangs deliver enough venom to kill an elephant . . . or 20 adult humans.

The king cobra (*Ophiophagus hannah*) can't shake your hand, but it can easily raise its head high enough to look you straight in the eyes (pictured). This super-sized and highly venomous reptile, which is also called the hamadryad, slithers throughout Southeast Asia and India. On average, king cobras measure 12 to 15 feet in length. A specimen caught in Negri Sembilan (now Malaysia) in 1937 was much larger. After being taken to the London Zoo (UK), this snake grew to a length of 18 feet, 9 inches, earning the Guinness World Records title of **Longest Venomous Snake** in the process.

Most Dangerous Bee

Record Holder:	Africanized honeybee
Place:	From South to North America

In 1957, a beekeeper accidentally released a bunch of highly aggressive African queen bees into Brazil. Oops! The bees bred with local species, forming a new strain known as the Africanized honeybee (*Apis mellifera scutellata*). These insects fiercely protect their territories up to a radius of 0.5 miles, attacking at the slightest threat. An attack swarm can inflict a fatal number of stings within minutes. The Africanized honeybee's venom is not more powerful than a normal bee. However, unlike other bees, this one doesn't lose its stinger (see magnified photo). This insect keeps on stinging again and again, injecting its poison each time, until its victim is dead or fled out of range. This deadly ability earned the Africanized honeybee the nickname "killer bee" — and the Guinness World Records title of **Most Dangerous Bee**.

Bee-ing Me

Many humans have gotten up close and personal with bees. Check out these Guinness World Record-breaking encounters.

- **Most Bees in the Mouth** — Dr. Norman Gary (USA) held 109 honeybees in his closed mouth for 10 seconds on October 20, 1998, in Los Angeles, California.

- **Most Bee Stings Removed** — On January 28, 1962, Johannes Relleke survived the stings of 2,443 bees at the Kamativi tin mine at Gwaii River in Wankie District, Zimbabwe (then Rhodesia). All of the stingers were removed and counted.

EXTREME FACTS

Killer bees are heading your way! Since 1957, when the strain first emerged, Africanized honeybees have been spreading north in the USA at a rate of about 1 mile per day. Today, these insects are common in the US border states of Texas, New Mexico, Arizona, and California. Other warm-weather areas are their next destinations.

Most Dangerous Glowing Animal

Record Holder:	Scorpion
Place:	Worldwide

Turn to this book's special color photo section and see how brightly a scorpion shines in UV light.

EXTREME FACTS

Scorpions grow by shedding an old outer layer and forming a new, larger one. This process is called molting. Newly molted scorpions do not fluoresce. This ability returns gradually as a scorpion's brand-new outer layer hardens.

Did you know that all scorpions fluoresce, or glow in the dark, under certain conditions? The eerie effect occurs when ultraviolet light, which is invisible to the human eye, falls upon the scorpion's shell. It hits a special material called the hyaline layer that absorbs some of the light's energy. The lower-energy light bouncing back out from the scorpion is blue — and easily visible to any scorpion-searching human carrying an ultraviolet light source. Better watch out for the scorpion's venomous sting, though. This is, after all, the **Most Dangerous Glowing Animal** on our planet.

CHAPTER 6

Lifestyles of the Wild and Free

All of the creatures in this chapter are living on the edge, and that's just the way they like it! Come with us as we explore Nature's most extreme animal lifestyles. You'll claw your way into the bustling center of a crab "supercity," take a 10-year flight with a sensational seabird, sink into the ocean's depths with an octopus smarter than its name, and much more. Exhausted? Wrap up your adventures by taking a nap with one of our planet's sleepiest (*yawn*) mammals.

Longest Feathers in a Wild Bird Species

Record Holder:	Reeves's pheasant
Place:	China

See the air brake action by Reeves's pheasant in this book's special color photo section.

EXTREME FACTS

A British naturalist named John Reeves discovered this long-tailed pheasant in 1831 and shipped the first specimens back to his English homeland.

Imagine dragging an oversized feather duster behind you, every moment of every day. This is the inconvenient lifestyle of Reeves's pheasant (*Syrmaticus reevesii*), which owns the **Longest Feathers in a Wild Bird Species**. The central tail feathers of this Chinese bird can exceed 8 feet in length. That's a lot of extra baggage to carry around, but this bird has found an excellent use for its plumage. When escaping predators, this bird spreads its fantastic feathers and "brakes" in mid-air, allowing it to quickly change its flight path.

They're Having a Big Hair Day

Aaron Studham knows a thing or two about gargantuan body-hair growth. This American proudly sports the **Tallest Mohican** ever attempted (pictured)! Aaron's mighty Mohawk poked a full 21 inches off his scalp when measured in Leominster, Massachusetts, USA, on September 11, 2005.

More down-to-earth and longer is the hair belonging to China's Xie Qiuping. Her terrific tresses were 18 feet, 5.54 inches long when measured on May 8, 2004. Xie has been growing her hair since 1973, when she was 13 years old. Today, she boasts the **Longest Hair** of any human on Earth.

EXTREME FACTS

The magnificent feathers of the Reeves's pheasant are often used in theatrical costumes. They are especially popular in the Beijing Opera, which is one of the biggest companies in this bird's native China.

Most Airborne Bird

Record Holder:	Sooty tern
Place:	Tropical oceans worldwide

When it comes to flying, one bird knows how to live the high life! Found throughout the world's equatorial regions, young sooty terns (*Sterna fuscata*) take to the air as soon as their wings are developed enough for flight. They head out to sea and stay aloft for the next 3 to 10 years, thereby earning the Guinness World Records title of **Most Airborne Bird** (pictured). During their oceangoing years, sooty terns often live in large flocks. These flocks feed by swooping down and plucking fish from the sea. Individual birds will settle on the ocean's surface for a quick rest, taking off again as soon as they feel refreshed. The fantastic flight ends at adulthood, when a sooty tern returns to land to breed and create a new generation of record-breaking birds.

Most Aquatic Spider

Record Holder:	Diving bell spider
Place:	Asia, Europe, and Africa

The diving bell spider or water spider (*Argyroneta aquatica*) breathes air, not water. Yet this amazing arachnid spends nearly its entire life submerged in the ponds of Asia, Europe, and northern Africa. How does the world's **Most Aquatic Spider** breathe underwater? The spider uses dense hairs on its legs and abdomen to trap a bubble, or "diving bell," of oxygen (pictured). Whenever it needs to take a breath, the arachnid dips into its personal reservoir. The diving bell spider doesn't work too hard to maintain its air bubble. The bubble renews itself most of the time, absorbing oxygen from the water and releasing carbon dioxide like a mini handheld "lung." If the air-supply runs low, the spider makes a quick trip to the surface to refill its own, naturally created diving tank.

Longest Column of Ants

Record Holder:	Army ant and driver ant
Place:	Central and South America, and Africa

EXTREME FACTS

Army ants and driver ants work as groups to overcome obstacles. They use their bodies as building blocks, clinging to each other to form living bridges over streams, across holes in the ground, and up into trees.

Hup, two, three, four! That could be the motto of the army ants (genus *Eciton*) of Central and South America and the driver ants (genus *Dorylus*) of Africa. These insects spend their entire lives on the move, marching together in colonies up to 328 feet long and over 3 feet wide. That's the **Longest Column of Ants** formed by any species. A single column can contain as many as 600,000 individuals and take several hours to pass by. Enjoy the parade — but don't get too close. These ants are fierce hunters, attacking and eating any animal they encounter on their long-distance hikes.

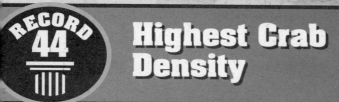

RECORD 44

Highest Crab Density

Record Holder:	Red crab
Place:	Christmas Island

About 14 million people live in the world's busiest human city. That sounds like a lot, but it's a mere drop in the bucket compared to the number of red crabs (*Gecarcoidea natalis*) that swarm Christmas Island in the Indian Ocean each year. From November to December, 120 million of these crustaceans crawl out of their forest burrows and head for the coast of their 52-square-mile island home (pictured). That works out to about one crab per square meter, giving this population explosion the **Highest Crab Density** of any gathering on the planet. Let's hope the participants don't get too *crabby* with their millions of neighbors!

RECORD 45

Deepest Octopus

Record Holder: Dumbo octopus
Place: Deep seas worldwide

Fly upside down with the dumbo octopus in this book's special color photo section.

EXTREME FACTS

Dumbo octopuses are named for the two earlike fins that stick out of their heads, much like the flapping ears of the famous cartoon elephant. These octopuses swim by moving their fins, pulsing their webbed arms, or pushing water through a funnel for jet propulsion.

Most octopuses enjoy the sunny, warm waters near the ocean's surface. But the members of the *Grimpoteuthis genus* have chosen a much more challenging lifestyle. Known collectively as dumbo octopuses, these 8-inch-long mollusks live at depths of up to 5,000 feet, close to the ocean floor. This species is the record-holder for **Deepest Octopus** known to science. Because its body is soft and gelatinous, the dumbo octopus is able to survive its habitat's enormous water pressure pushing against its body every second.

Sleepiest Marsupial

Record Holder:	Koala
Place:	Australia

Tired, tired, tired. That's the best way to describe the koala (*Phascolarctos cinereus*), which has a well-deserved reputation as the world's **Sleepiest Marsupial** (pictured). This Guinness World Record-holder snoozes away 18 out of 24 hours every day! The koala's extreme exhaustion is due to its low-energy diet, which consists of about 1.3 to 1.7 pounds of eucalyptus leaves daily. In energy terms, that's the equivalent of a human eating only one bowl of cereal during each 24-hour period. You'd probably hit the snooze button a few times, too, if you had to survive on such slim pickings.

Better Than a Mug Shot

In 1997, scientists discovered that even koalas have fingerprints. Koala prints have ridges and patterns that are similar to those found on human prints. Koala prints can be traced to a specific marsupial, just as human fingerprints are unique to one person. Scientists are excited about this breakthrough because, although fingerprints are common among primates, it is rare to find fingerprints made by the rest of the animal kingdom. Koalas possibly developed this trait because they use their hands and feet to grasp food, similar to primates. Animals with similar habits often develop similar body features.

CONCLUSION

The Journey Continues

Although our safari ends here, you can keep exploring the world's most extreme animals, people, and the stories behind the history-making facts. Continue your journey among the online archives (*www.guinnessworldrecords.com*) and within the pages of *Guinness World Records* at your local library or bookstore. You're guaranteed to find thousands of records covering all things big, small, long, short, least, most, and many other sensational superlatives.

Interested in making history by having your own record? Check out the official guidelines on how to become a record-breaker, featured on the next page. Maybe your name will appear in the next edition of the record books!

BE A RECORD-BREAKER!

Message from the Keeper of the Records:

Record-breakers are the ultimate in one way or another — the youngest, the oldest, the tallest, the smallest. So how do you get to be a record-breaker? Follow these important steps:

1. Before you attempt your record, check with us to make sure your record is suitable and safe. Get your parents' permission. Next, contact one of our officials by using the record application form at *www.guinnessworldrecords.com.*

2. Tell us about your idea. Give us as much information as you can, including what the record is, when you want to attempt it, where you'll be doing it, and other relevant information.

a) We will tell you if a record already exists, what safety guidelines you must follow during your attempt to break that record, and what evidence we need as proof that you completed your attempt.

b) If your idea is a brand-new record nobody has set yet, we need to make sure it meets our requirements. If it does, then we'll write official rules and safety guidelines specific to that record idea and make sure all attempts are made in the same way.

3. Whether it is a new or existing record, we will send you the guidelines for your selected record. Once you receive these, you can make your attempt at any time. You do not need a Guinness World Record official at your attempt. But you do need to gather evidence. Find out more about the kind of evidence we need to see by visiting our website.

4. Think you've already set or broken a record? Put all of your evidence as specified by the guidelines in an envelope and mail it to us at Guinness World Records.

5. Our officials will investigate your claim fully — a process that can take a few weeks, depending on the number of claims we've received and how complex your record is.

6. If you're successful, you will receive an official certificate that says you are now a Guinness World Record-holder!

Need more info? Check out *www.guinnessworldrecords.com* for lots more hints, tips, and some top record ideas. Good luck!

PHOTO CREDITS

9 Scorpion © f1 online/Alamy; 11 Aye-aye © David Haring/OSF/Photolibrar 12, 24 Shark art © Khrameshina Tatiana/Shutterstock; 13, 59 Snorkeler art, 74 Octopus art © Sabri Deniz Kizil/Shutterstock; 14 Komodo dragon © Cyril Ruoso/ MindenPictures; 15 Reticulated python © Compost/Peter Arnold Inc.; 16 Capybar © John Waters/Nature Picture Library; 18 Leech © Hans Reinhard/Bruce Coleman Inc.; 20 Stick insect art © Eric Isselée/Shutterstock; 21, 66 Scorpion art, 42 Snake art © OzZon/Shutterstock; 22 Dean Sheldon © Richard Bradbury/Guinness Worl Records; 23 Octopus © Dario Sabljak/Shutterstock; 25-26, 54 Frog art © angel digital/Shutterstock; 27 Howler monkey © Arco Images GmbH/Alamy; 28 Ratel © Ho New/Reuters; 30, 48 Squid art, 37 Polar bear art © Shutterstock; 32 Polar be © An Scott/Shutterstock; 33 Butterfly art, Caterpillar art © Markov/Shutterstock 34, 62, 68 Bird art © Myper/Shutterstock; 35 Viperfish © Paltzner/blickwinkel/ Alamy; 36 Polar bear © Therin-Weise/Arco Images/Alamy; 37 Seal art, 51-52, 72 An art © Michelle Martinez Design; 38 Mole art © Potapov Alexander/Shutterstock; 39 Roadrunner © Panoramic Images/Getty Images; 40 Peregrine falcon © Galen Rowell/Peter Arnold Inc.; 41 Falcon art © Princess Lola/Shutterstock; 43 Jackie Bibby © Ellis Neel,Alamogordo Daily News/AP Photo; 44 Squid Eye © Andrew Kerr/Shutterstock; 45 Fish art © John David Bigl III/Shutterstock; 46 Narwhal © Paul Nicklen/National Geographic/Getty Images; 47 Unicorn art © Norma Cornes Shutterstock; 50 Giant armadillo © Gabriel Rojo/NPL/Minden Pictures; 53 Aardvar © Anthony Bannister/Animals Animals; 55 Fish art © Vasilkin/Shutterstock; 56 Victor "Larry" Gomez © John Wright/Guinness World Records; 57 Piranha © Peter Jochems/Shutterstock; 58 Piranha teeth © Seapics.com; 59 Piranha art © Dawn Hudson/Shutterstock; 60 Puffer fish art © Maggie/Shutterstock; 61 Leopar seal © Tim Davis/Corbis; 63 King cobra © Simon King/Nature Picture Library; 64 Killer bee stinger © Dr. Dennis Kunkel/Visuals Unlimited, Swarm © Premaphoto Nature Picture Library; 65 Bee art © Robert Adrian Hillman/Shutterstock; 67 Ants Christopher Tan Teck Hean/Shutterstock; 69 Aaron Studham © Newscom; 70 Soot tern © Kerstin Hinze/Nature Picture Library; 71 Diving bell spider © WILDLIFE/Pete Arnold Inc.; 73 Red crabs © Jurgen Freund/Nature Picture Library; 75 Koala © Mart Harvey/Peter Arnold Inc.; 76 Fingerprint art © Dmitry Terentjev/Shutterstock.